Snap Shots:

Photo Op Poems from an Everyday Life

For Bethlane —
New friend,
Kindred Spirit —

Hugs,
Rochelle

By Rochelle Brener

To Carl,
Who is the rock-solid support
Behind anything significant I do.

To Barry,
Who (admirably) lives his own Truth.

To Karen,
A woman of courage,
Who I want to be like
When I grow up.

And to Samantha,
Beauty Writer.

CrystalWings Publishing
xtalwings@aol.com

All Rights Reserved
ISBN: 0-9717833-0-6

Photography by Rochelle Brener
Book Design by Karen Conway,
Conway Creations
www.conwaycreations.com

Snap Shots:

Photo Op Poems from
an Everyday Life

By Rochelle Brener

Table of Contents

Forward

I have long been fascinated with the kind of poetry that tells stories. For me, poetry often serves as a verbal photo. And in that poetry — usually evoked by sensuous colors, sounds, smells — flashes of character development may reside.

I can remember sitting on my grandmother's front porch glider, a child of maybe nine or ten, printing poems in a bound composition book. They usually made some sense, they had rhythm and they almost always rhymed. As an English major in college in the mid-sixties, the esoteric poetic ramblings of e.e. cummings and the crazy-making poetry of Allen Ginsberg and his ilk left me finger-snappingly cold. Give me a poem that said something I could follow, and I was happy.

Then, somewhere between college and graduate school, fourteen years and life happened. By then, I had spent countless hours behind the lens of a camera, as a photojournalist and a fine arts photographer. And I had continued to write my poems. In that time, the poetry and the photos came together, although not yet in a meaningful way. I had developed an appreciation for the "esoterics," even coming to love some of their work. I learned, somehow, to *feel* the stories inside the words, even if I didn't get all the references.

Toward the end of the eighties, I had the opportunity to attend a workshop given by the late Allen Ginsberg (yes, I *had* come a long way by then), dealing with the concept of "snapshot poetics," (Ginsberg's label). His class (and an interview he granted me after the class), cleared some of the fog. I came to realize that poetry had few rights or wrongs anymore. What it has is wonderful, juicy words and understandability. With that in my pocket, I wrote my way through an MFA in Writing (Vermont College), gathering kudos and criticism for my photographic poems.

Somewhere along the line, I discovered expressive arts therapy. "Aha," I thought, "a practical use for this stuff!" Meanwhile, I was also off and running as a psychotherapist and as the Founder/Director of Mandala Center for Creative Wellness®, an alternative health care center, so for a time, my own writing took a back burner. I wrote poetry less frequently — but I still wrote — usually articles for *SPIRAL MAGAZINE*, a regional bi-monthly focusing on holistic practice and wellness.

It was in this period of time that I had the pleasure of reading two important books by author/artist/world visionary Jan Phillips. *Marry Your Muse* reminded me that I had always been on the right track; I went back to writing poetry. *God Is at Eye Level: Photography as a Healing Art* slammed it home — that whether I was behind a camera or in front of a keyboard, I was still writing — in other words, still creating. For me, there was no separation between the writing of a poem and the recognition and taking of a good photo.

I offer special thanks to Margaret M. Eck, my good friend and coordinator at Mandala Center for Creative Wellness®, for her patience and prudence as proofreader, and for her encouragement as well. Also to Marilyn Day, founder of WomanWords, a cluster group of the International Women's Writing Guild based at Mandala Center in Albany, NY, for reading and offering feedback; and to Jan Phillips for doing the same; and to Judy Prest, whose poetic work *Sailing on Spirit Wind,* is an inspiration and a delight.

It Isn't the Camera That Steals Your Soul

The ancient ones knew the box-on-three-legs
was a one-eyed demon. One blink and its brain
would explode, and in the smoke it would fish
your soul out of your mouth, leaving a shell
that was supposed to be you, while the real you
stayed stuck on its glass plate tongue.

That's what the ancients knew. We know the camera
is for marking history: wars, weddings, babies,
bar mitzvahs. There's Bubbe and Great-Uncle Heshy
rubbing back and forth over time, growing mildewed
in someone's basement, wearing thin in someone's attic.
Age and heat keeps them together. If you separate them,
they will tear each other's faces off; they never got along
when they were alive, either.

Cousin Marty, there's the picture I was looking for!
See? That's really what he looked like, beard and all.
He used to sit and watch people for hours, staring
straight into them, as if he could see to their core. Then
he'd go back to his room and you could hear the tap-tap
of his old Underwood. He never said what he was doing.
Then, some years later, he gave everyone in the family
this book for Chanukah. We opened it up and looked;
pretty soon there one of us would be, in a poem. Every
one of us, and other people too; people we didn't know
and people we didn't want to know.

If any of us had realized Marty was a poet, he'd have
warned the others to wear reflecting sunglasses
and to keep their mouths shut. We all know it:
it isn't the camera that steals your soul,
it's the poet.

A Grim Fairy Tale

You had a certain grace about you,
a gentility. Soul, I guess
you could call it, warm
in the center.

You were to me like crystal wind-chimes
on summer nights, a shiny presence
from some children's story
much read and loved.

You invited me into your dream world,
and I moved toward the entrance,
fantasizing forever. But you
ended the story quickly, slammed
the book shut, and ran away.

There is no Prince Charming,
said the Frog.

Lovers in the Mirror

The house next door to St. Mary's was a ruin,
but she bought it because of the mirror each previous owner
had left, attached forever to the living room wall —
eight feet of silvered glass, framed wide with
gilt turns and figures that subtly suggested
the positions of lovers in *The Joy of Sex.*

Dressing in front of it, her sculpted legs
danced their female poses, her dress
creating a scarlet swirl around her knees
as she turned smoothly side to side, checking
her image, pleased to look so well, glad
to be over him at last, happy that the mirror
couldn't talk about all it had seen,
from the nights it had gleamed reflected gaslight
in the whorehouse parlor to the candlelit
lovemaking on her living room sofa just months ago.

An unexpected frown mars her face, like a black cat
intersecting her path. She backs away, stops,
steals in close to the mirror, slowly as a predator
moving in for a kill. Carefully she tilts
her head back, squints, sees through dark lashes
the blur of lovers — him, someone facelessly new
— making promises as he had with her.

The truth was, he had promised nothing. She only felt
as though he had. He had warned her, she reminds herself
now, of a past with too many lovers. She thought then, he'd
never found the right one. She knew now,
his game was conquest. Kill, and move on.
Suddenly she sees them both, tangled bodies
and sweated sheets, a mass of gold surrounding them.
In the center, his silver ghost arms come alive,

engulf her — remembered feelings, fingers playing
on breasts. The image does a kaleidoscope turn
and she sees him with other lovers, other times,
other women reflected in the mirror.
They take shape, move from the baroque frame
into his arms. His body becomes
an endless part of the glass; he will not be gone.
She watches in agonized fascination as he grasps,
plunges, releases. She gathers her breath
into her diaphragm and turns away, turns back,
moves slowly, reluctantly takes her destined place
at the edge of the frame, one more figure in gilt.

Commuter Flight 3410 Out of Newark

Eight passengers eye each other
as they wait to board the plane on the runway
just outside gate 2A East at the North Terminal.
Over the gate, two words: Emergency Exit.

Thirteen seats is not a good omen. One woman
enters the plane, looks out at the wing, sees
"To oil, see flight manual page 453." She blanches,
turns and runs. The copilot smirks.

The wing is sheet metal screwed together
by the lowest bidder; some skin is peeling back
near the motor. The passengers try to distribute
their weight evenly as they board.

The pilot himself pulls the door shut once, succeeds
in closing on the second try. The copilot asks if
she should push this button first or last; her voice
loud and nasal and pure Brooklyn.

A man with patches of hair missing from the back
of his head clutches a rosary. The Sister
whose thighs drip over the sides of her seat
grips the handle of her attaché case

and moves her lips as she stares out the window,
watching the ground fall away. The plane
seems to be racing a cloud formation off the right
wing and can't outrun it.

An elderly woman in a rear seat purses
and unpurses her lips. An executive type strikes
a conversation with the ash blonde across the aisle;
their talk hums with the motor and blends

into the wind sucking through the overhead vents
that will not close. The old woman falls asleep,
her knotted fingers picking at the rayon flowers
printed on the folds of her dress. She dreams of
black smoke, and earth spinning closer.

5

The Bride Doll

When I look at her, I smell October and
think of the woman who made her, stitched
her lace tier upon tier, patience
and practice guiding her hands. She works
in her tiny shop on the side going up
Hunter Mountain, a white stone building
almost hidden by autumn's sunny frenzy
of afternoon color. She introduces
her husband, a gnarling man of eighty, bent
like the arthritic tree outside
the front door.

He is proud of this woman, his wife. What a catch
he'd made, some twenty years back. "He takes
good care of me," she says, as he rides his bowed legs
outside, to chop some old cherry wood for the stove,
"though I worry what I'll do when he goes."
She sighs, hands stilled, silent in her lap.
She sits, surrounded
by lace dolls and twilight.

Apricot

Anonymous cat sunning on a stone sill,
I want to feed you nuggets as sweet
as the amber of your eyes. I reach up
to scratch behind your calico ears,
but you turn, lick my hand
with a tongue as rough as apricot skin,
look at me as if to say
"Don't be absurd. I've been here
chewing on sunshine pulp all day."

Tomhannock

Last summer I fished the Tomhannock. Its
taunting inhabitants porpoised the water
near the rocks under the bridge, playing
just out of range of my longest cast.
The heat bounced from the embrace of trees
that surround the reservoir and shield it
from Route 40. Sunlight shone pink crystal
from the scales of strawberry bass. Walleye
and largemouth, perch and tiger-muskie
swam away from jighead and Mister Twister
as if they had been insulted by such
simple fare. Night snuck in
and I watched the sun lose its lazy red battle
on the other side of the water.

Now, it is almost winter. A darkness
as still as my dead grandfather lays its hand
over the water. The Coleman
by my side whispers its propane;
its light marks the boundary between
liquid and solid. Elm and poplar move
as if I and not the wind had jostled them.
They send down dead leaves that sound like rain
and clot the shoreline.

I sneak under the bridge as if I was a spy
with information for the enemy. The moon
offers a disk of weak white, slips it over
the horizon, divides the water into light and dark,
yin and yang. I cast my lure and it flies
into a blackness so secure I can't even see
the end of my pole. Three feet beyond
the plunk of my luredrop, there is
no sound of rippling water.

There's a no-man's-land
where the ebony meets the mirror.
Trees and hills pose opposite me, silhouettes
reflected in the hardening liquid.
In the cold, nothing moves.

An Unfortunately Ordinary Love Fable

She was prepared for him to tell her
that they would talk it over; they
could work it out like they always did.
She could hardly wait
to hear his truck throbbing
in the driveway, could almost smell
the tang of his cologne, feel the scratch
of his beard as his mouth touched
her neck, brushed the skin
between her breasts just last night
before the ugly words and
the awful slap.

He would kiss the space again where
her heart beat hard, belying her false calm.
She spent the day regretting her words,
rehearsing new ones, shopping for
something special to wear, debating
which costume might be right for
"forgive me." How should she say it:
frilly, feminine and subservient (as
he thought she should be)? Outrageous
and funky? Blatant, fuck-me sexual? She
decided to be herself: straightforward, satin
and female. Honesty was, after all,
best for apologies.

She walked home by way of the park, pleased
with her purchases. He liked her in satin, though
she didn't much fancy it herself. He liked
gladiolas and chicken roasted and Blue Nun, though
wine made her queasy. Walking, she smiled as
she saw his truck. The last thought
that came to her was that they had bought it
together. She raised her hand to wave,
saw the redhead with him, close enough
to be more than casual. It hit her
with all the force of his one-ton
pick-up, spun her around.

She felt her left arm thrown onto Delaware Ave,
her right leg tossed as far as State Street. Her hair
curled round Washington Park as her head
exploded. A hand reached out to their home
up route 5. Her heart felt like it had been
dragged all the way to upper Central, deposited
on her own doorstep, still beating
though she didn't know why.
He sped down the road in the old
primer red-and-white, blasting
Brenda Lee's version of "Who's Sorry Now"
out the open wide windows. Before
he turned the corner, she saw
the message spitprinted in the mud
that chronically crusted the tailgate:
good-bye.

She didn't understand
the feeling of relief.

Confession of a Stoned Poet

"Poetry is a prism of words."
— Carl Sandburg

The light over my desk is merciless, a white hot
diamond covering my paper in glare.
The page reflects the words I write, and
I need to soften some truth that hurts my heart
and makes my eyes run.

I cover the lamp with a deep blue square of silk,
hoping to bring my words to the softness
of faded denim, but the blue is too dark, turns
my fingernails to bottled ink spilled accidentally,
spreading over my paper, over the desk, over the rug,

going everywhere but where it should. I change
the bulb to some party-light green
and it casts a jade hand across the page.
My true hand turns the color of
some grotesque alien life form and I
give up the bulb in order to keep dinner down.

I switch to a red bulb, pilfered
from my old darkroom, and immediately I think sex,
rubies in January snow, blood. I consider
my current state of affairs: right now, blood
or lust would be better in my life
than in a poem. I could write about it
after, maybe.

There's a yellow bug light on the porch
and I snatch it, screw it into the lamp over my desk;
but its color jaundices my outlook
as well as the paper I scrawl across.
I look at it and wonder how lawyers
can keep a straight face,

constantly peering at their foolscap
and fighting to free murderous clients, who go out
and commit more murder, leaving blood
in the snow on the streets. A soft pink bulb
gives my paper a gentler cast.
It's what I'd want

for entertaining old ladies at tea. My hand
scribes pink all over the page, but
the richness of opal and white fire is gone.
I put the white bulb back in, treasuring
its brilliance, its relentless glare
that mirrors my words back into my eyes.

i knew a poet once
(after lyn lifshin)

her hair flew out
in every direction   and
she saw   black apples
sex in onion rings   madonnas
in heat   things that
no one else could see   thought
in image-lists
attacked her prey   with
sensuous lust
and a felt-tip pen   till
it was lying red
scrawled   all over
the page   she'd wake
before dawn   before heat
write   for hours   before her feet
inched out of the covers
forgetting   there was a sunrise
slept   with a spiral notebook
on the other side of the double bed
as if   it were her lover

13

After All This Time

So what do we expect from each other now? Gratitude?
If anything, it might be repayment in kind; I dealt you out
a good share of pain, once I caught on to your game. And
the truth is, I couldn't say right now exactly which cards
I dealt from the bottom on purpose,
and which came up as consequence.

Tell me where anger goes when it's lived inside too long.
Never mind, I'll tell you. It turns into a granite joker that
never erodes. It teaches you to cry inward,
to form a skin of vinegar ice, to nourish the rot
seeded deep at the core. If you could catch the tears,
they would be bitter wine, meant to be drunk straight,
like hemlock, in a fast interval of real sorrow
and true mourning for the cards that you dealt me,
and badly.

Twenty-Fifth Anniversary

Nothing grows here but the emptiness.

It's icebergs that collide, slow motion,
move together, combine. They grind
their hips into each other,
shatter deliberately, become
what it must have been like
in the Ice Age.

Silence flies past in days of cold wind
and nothing said. Ice blankets our souls,
covers our universe. Whoever speaks first
might crack it, letting frozen monsters out
for others to see. We barely breathe;
the chill is already exploding our lungs.

The house we share fights the summer sun.
Central air maintains the mood. Closed
white drapes tell the world to go away.
Everything's gone frigid, noiseless.

Nothing grows here but the emptiness.

2 A.M.
Daylight Savings Ends Its Shift

I open the window wide though the autumn night
sends its crushed cold moaning through the last
of the leaves that clutch the trees
with skeletal strength. Silence stops the wind:
a last moment of respect.

All the wind-gods watch in awe as the sky laments
the sun; big tears pat-pat blues music
against the leaves spread across the grass
like a crunch of dead carpet.

I change to the comfort of old flannel
and tell the clock by the bed to wait an extra hour
for daylight. One hour, more or less,
shouldn't matter, unless you're waiting.

Summer is Only Sounds,
Pressing Heat

We knew it would come, yet it breaks
sudden on us, like a telescope
of green bursting full from Spring.
Trees are instantly dense with heat;
languid drooping leaves crave the breeze
that makes them jitterbug in the air,
butterflies caught on stems. Somewhere
a newborn squalls, a tiny cry
almost invisible in the chatter of peepers
and cicadas. Bees hum their own melody,
interrogating pollen from flowers,
oblivious to the sun. Butter melts
in its dish on the counter where I left it,
like Sambo's tiger. The swelter
has a weight of its own. It presses
on my chest like the body of a lover —
the one I want when he's gone
and want gone when he's here.

Spiritual

Naked, at summer's full blue moon, she moves through
the Tai Chi, gathering energy, burning sage and sweetgrass
in an abalone shell. A polished moonstone is tucked
under her tongue, inviting visions as she dances.
Her hair glides down her back, slides over her arms.
She acknowledges each of the directions in its turn
and eagle feathers begin to float from the ceiling.
She moves desperately now, her breath deepening
to the roar of wind. The feathers float around her,
and she thanks Buddha, God, Allah, the Great Mother,
Father Sky, and all the Powers-That-Be.

She puts on the dress she has been saving for ceremonies,
though it outlines her nakedness. Barefoot, she goes outside
to look at the faces in the dark moon, to hear the clouds
scrape the sky. Her toes begin to itch, then grow roots
and spread deep into the ground, a sudden connection
that makes her ache in a way her husband never could.
The crystal around her neck grows hot; its silver wire
wrapping burns against the grain of her skin, grain
that roughens and turns to white bark. She puts her hands
to her mouth, covering her silent O-shaped scream of amazement
against the insistent power of her communing. A breeze answers
her cry and branches sprout from her arms, her hair. Leaves drip
with the tears of late August night-heat.

In the morning, her sons use the garden hose to water her roots.
They tell her ex-husband that their job is to tend Mother Earth.
He doesn't understand, mutters obscenities about a woman
who abandons her children, and tells the boys that they'll have to
live with him, the courts will see to that. He unzips
and relieves himself against her body before he forces the boys
into his car.

Laughter in All the Right Places

She watches Donna Reed repromise in late night
black-and-white, Nick at Night,
all the clichés that go with turning forty, watches
Harriet Nelson infer that two cars, charge accounts, two
perfect children in suburban-perfect schools were
the inevitable rewards for all good girls. June Cleaver
is a co-conspirator; even her parents had showered her
with tales of castles in the country. Television ads promised
white knights to do the laundry, and men in small boats
to tend the moat of her toilet tank.

She had taken seriously these shirt-waisted,
Florida-swampland con artists, believed them all,
just as she had trusted *Seventeen Magazine*'s promises
that laughter in all the right places and Revlon's daring
new Persian Melon lipstick would cast a spell
over her own personal prince. Then she would marry,
have babies (in that order), graduate to *Ladies' Home Journal*
and *Redbook*. She swallowed it, a magic wafer
that all the boys swallowed too; taken as gospel
according to Ozzie Nelson, Jim Anderson, Ward Cleaver.

No one had thought then, of women's lib, of burning bras
(they should have burned diapers, she mused), of
a fifty-four percent divorce rate. No one warned her
that the man the ads sold as "Mr. Right" could
steal her soul, batter her with obscenities
more vile than body blows, leave her
scarred beyond all thought of healing.

She reaches out, remotely obliterating the liars
with the touch of a button. Alone in her house, the last vestige
of old promises, she stretches across a mile of comforter,

19

turns off the lamp. Settling under expensive down, feeling
uneasily safe for one more night, she half wishes she could
join the rest of the world, go half-crazy or live half-crazed.
Instead, tomorrow she will put on her strength
like the worn out apron (a gift from her mother)
that she hangs like guilt on the back of the pantry door,
and bake some chocolate chip cookies
for no one in particular.

Or, maybe tomorrow, she'd put the castle up for sale.

Reunion

I said goodbye at seven
to the child whose uncle's body
ripped soft flesh, made blood run,
and caught, blamed her enticing
green eyes, sensuous lips.
I left her alone, crying in corners,
learning the hardness of feeling
nothing one day at a time. I left her
setting like plaster in a mold, learning
smart words and tight laughter. She grew
into someone disappearing in distances,
connected to me by a length of sinew
so fragile I knew one day it could break.
Tonight I saw her again, my eyes
reflecting themselves in a dark window.
Nothing will change for anyone else, but
now I hold her close to my heart,
mother to myself.

Ghost

I can't close your door. It's as if
your bedroom calls out to me, tries to coax me in
by some slant of my own imagination. I peek in
and see the melange of clothes — black (your Gothic color),
white, yellow, hot pink, purple — that cascade
from your closet and tumble across the floor
like laughter caught in a waterfall. The rest
of your space is a fiesta of Conté crayons,
acrylic paints, sketch pads, cassette tapes.

I give in, go inside as if your room demanded it
and I was powerless to say no. I can smell
the combination of old Nikes, paint thinner, Lutece,
as if you'd left only minutes ago to cruise the mall
with your friends. Days like this I stand in the midst
of your girl-turning-woman debris in the afternoon sun
that pours itself through the window as if ordered to do so
by Ra, the sun-god of crossword puzzles. It warms the spot
where you used to sit on the rug and sketch.

I don't touch a thing, don't pick up, don't clean.
I only look, look and breathe you in, turn a full slow circle
and leave. I mean to close your door, but I never do.
Every day, like ritual, your room calls me. Even empty,
it's still full of you.

Don't Think of an Elephant

When you tell yourself not to think,
or to think of nothing, it's amazing
what your mind will do. Like when
someone says, "don't think of
an elephant" and all you can conjure up
are Dumbo ears and peanut breath.

Some experts tell you, "don't blame
yourself," and right away you're in
trouble. You know that they mean
you have to look inside yourself
and see what it was you should have done
instead of whatever it was
you did.

So, you spread your if-onlies out
on the table like a game of solitaire
and then rearrange the cards, looking
for some sort of ace to build on.
Go ahead. Try to cheat. Turn
the cards in your hand up
one by one.

When you played it straight,
it didn't work either.

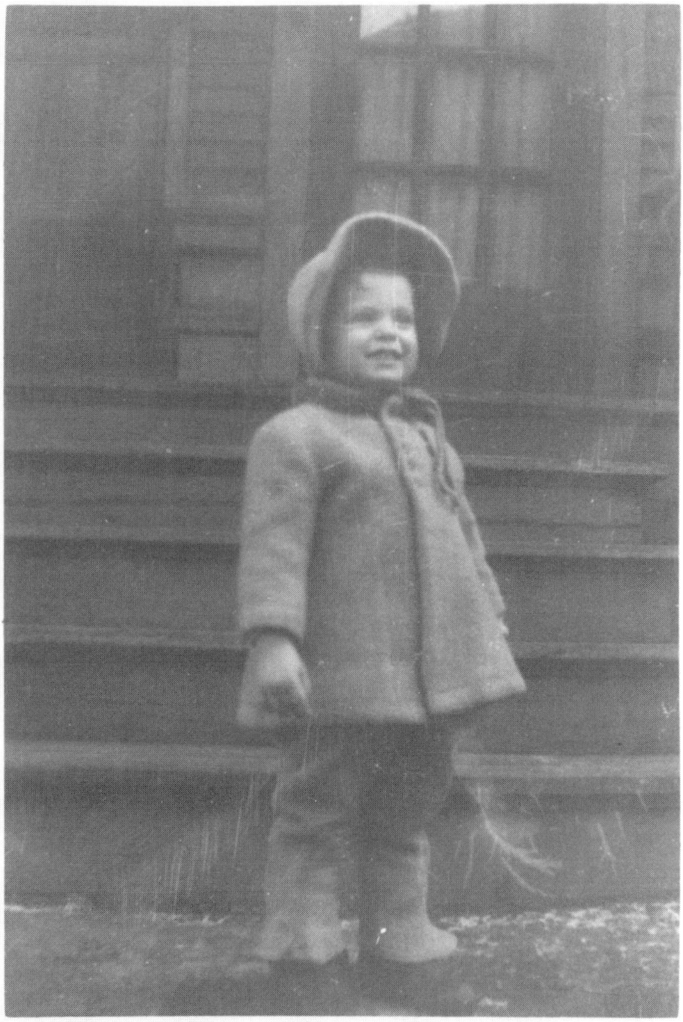

Photo by Cy Brener

Moving Day

I don't know this place; it isn't mine.
All I can see are boxes bigger than I am, boxes
marked with *my* black crayon that I never got back
and now it's lost and I only have seven left and
I don't know where those are, either.

Maybe in a box. Maybe in that one, but
I don't know. These boxes have a spy code on them
that grown-ups make up, and they mark it on
the boxes so I won't know where things are.

I figured out A and B and C and D and some of the rest,
but I don't know how to make the code, or how to
put it together so the code makes sense. If I knew
where my stuff went to, maybe I wouldn't be so scared.
I don't think I trust grown-ups any more.

I want to know what happened to my bed. It's blue
and has sides on it, and it's gone! And why
didn't Mrs. Goldstein come, too? I need her
to make my soup with chicken and slurpy noodles.
It tastes like hugs and the noodles are long
and slap on my chin.

She laughs when I tell her the right words to use
instead of the funny Yiddish-y ones
I think she makes up. I know she's old
because her hair is all gray, *that's* how I know!

These men I don't know keep going back and forth
to that truck, touching all our stuff. Daddy,
I need my panda and he only has one ear, so he
can't hear me call. My room is all the way in the back
— who will hear *me* call if monsters hide under my bed?

I'll spend the rest of my life in back rooms, crying,
and no one will come, no one
will hear. No one will save me.

New Orleans: Interview
With a Street Musician

bin playin this dam
alto sax   since ah bin a kid
figgered ah'd mek
some real toney music one day
and ah did
ah did   stardust an blue moon
an you tell me your dream
din't know them songs could wail blue
betcha   raaht?

man, that time was honey
pure sweet   ah squalled them tunes
so faahn them folks inna bars
would git all teary   but
it took ovah mah laahf
the music did   yeah
ah breathed it   slep it   ate it
hocked ev'rthing ah owned
jest ta keep playin   latsa tahms fer
nothin   jest drinks anna sanwich
but it was laahk a fix, y'know

some naahts wenna jammin got good
anna room fulla smoke
an people drinkin
an lovin the sounds ah made
set m'bones tuh achin whin it come taahm
tuh stop   shee-it,
made love tuh dat dam horn so long
it turned mah hair tuh whaat   fergot
what a steady woman was laahk
anna sax, man   made it all a good blow

got anotha butt there, man?

Facing Forty

She drags a kitchen chair around the table
to face the glass door. Rocking the chair
onto its back legs, she perversely puts a bare foot
up against the clean pane. My mother
would kill me for this, she giggles, trying to decide
whether it's funny, since she's thinking of
suicide anyway. She settles on ironic.
Seeing her naked reflection, she wonders
if she should have put on a robe before she came
downstairs to challenge the night
with only a chipped cup of leftover coffee
for ammunition.

Every night, she does this battle with
sleep, bedding down at a reasonable hour
(just like a human being) and rising at three to
wander the house like the living dead,
trying to remember good times there.
She stares at the other houses now, curious
to know if all the world's patio doors
are slid shut against this ceaseless heat,
summer's dripping air.

Like covered wagons circled for the night, the houses
back-to-back each other, their circle of yards forming
an O-shaped guard. Her mission now is simple:
advance through one more day, bind her wounds at night.
Cold coffee is plasma. From the open battleground,
the air conditioner grinds the heat up and pumps it
into the air she tries to breathe, until she is almost lulled into
believing that true comfort is a mere matter of
sixty-eight degrees inside and eighty-six out.
She peers past the sight of herself, the naked sentry
in the glass, wondering if anyone else is
staring into the clutch of backyards, keeping watch.

Some neighbor's windchime starts to tinkle
a tinny warning, but the breeze dies before it can attack
anything else. Maybe, she thinks, it was a ghost,
a gray slipping presence to remind her
of old laughter, of good days gone to rot.
She shivers off the thought that all her life
has turned to compost. She hates the constant invasion
of staccato gunfire repetition in her mind:
it wasn't
supposed
to be
this way.

In Light of What the Critics Say...
(Face It, Tootsie, You're No Dustin Hoffman)

The sick bile of last night's cast party
rises like the skyscrapers that
retch against Manhattan's clouds. Today
the director and producers sit like judges
across the proscenium arch, ready
to pass sentence. The actor's eyes
brush past theirs, stop just off audience left,
not daring to meet. The glare of the single spot
bores through him, offers no warmth,
like their stares.

Pretense is his life. He lives
the pollyanna'd half-truths of
Broadway musicals, hoping to make it,
lives any lie, fakes it. Suddenly
he goes cold, flop sweat trickling down
his sides inside his shirt, certain
that the story behind the script was
the life he lives. He wonders if he might have
whistled in the dressing room, had blown
his lines once too often, if he was
no longer capable of a
covering ad-lib.

He reminds himself to smile across the footlights,
offer whatever it might take to fix it, save himself.
Try all the charm of a stage-presence worn too often
off-stage, worn like an amulet with
no magic left in it. He knows that soon
he'll ask who he has to fuck to save
his role, and they'll all laugh.
He'll mean it, though.

The quiet intensity of an unembracing audience
remains in the theater like the stench
of old, bad sex. It casts
a visible mist across the orchestra pit, and
the actor shivers. The show will close
and again he will be as useless
as the dust at dawn in the city's streets.
The silence in the theater
is a rasp of torture
against the grain of skin.

Nightmare

The Demon of Energy sits, a parrot
heavy with color, on my shoulder, squawks
me into another wakeful night. I
wander the house in search of sleep,
but the Demon whispers obscenities,
ugly adjectives that conjure
his compatriots from midnight caverns.
Gremlins dance in mischiefed frenzy,
monsters make madness. The Witch
of Dark Adventures waits
at the windy corners of my mind, waits
for me to nod off, to disappear, so
her birds can circle my absence. The Sly Devil
swears he will do my dreams for me,
but, I argue, then the dreams
will not be mine! The Ghost of
Christmas Past lurks in my closet
to haunt happiness. Trolls have claimed
my underbed, believing the bulk
of brass and mattress to be their bridge.
I dare not walk around it. If I do,
they will reach out like my cat Tasha,
grab my ankle, and drag me under
to eat my soul and laugh,
like Bloody Bones.

The Shrine

She never got rid of it,
that old tapestry chair with
the faded cabbage roses, not
even after it went out of style, not
even after she gave its mate to the Salvation Army,
not even after the sun had rotted the fabric
and the stuffing began to ooze out
where his arms would have rubbed
if he'd lived to sit in it for twenty more years.

You could tell it was his, broken in
to his exact shape, antimacassars stained
from his hair tonic (men used it then). She
used to call it a "sight" and a "shame" and
threaten to have the trash men cart it away
one day when he was at work; but I was happy
to sit in it and wait, swallowed
by the overstuffed cushions, in the sundust
that spotlighted that throne, sometimes for hours,
until he came home at twilight.
I would sit quietly, breathing in
the Grandpa smell of Wildroot,
Camels and Aqua Velva, the evening paper
in my chubby fists already turned
to the funnies. In he'd walk, unbuttoning
his suit jacket as he strode across
the living room. Still I waited, in my
little-girl patience, almost holding my breath
as he loosened his tie, undid his vest. One shot
of whiskey to relax his voice, and one shot
just to sit at the ready on the table next to us,
and he was mine till dinner was ready.

His scent never left that chair.
Grandma sat in it only one time,
on the day she died.

When I Was Forty, Mother Told Me
Stories I Had Never Heard Before

I.

My father would sit in his favorite chair for hours,
One time for so long they had to call the doctor,
They couldn't tell for certain if he was even breathing.
They thought he had died, but of what, I don't know.
Maybe anger. He would do that after a fight with Ma,
Just sit, alone, seeing nothing, shredding bits of paper,
Cloth, anything that came to hand from the table
By his chair. One time he shredded his lighted Yarro
Cigar, not even noticing that he'd charred his fingernails.
He'd just sit, looking dead ahead at phantoms raging,
Remembering pogrom days, hearing the Polish and Rumanian ghosts
Praising the brave young Avram. I only remember him
Sitting alone in his chair in an empty new world, and
Ma wanting food for the eight of us that survived,
Maybe a new teapot, or winter gloves.

II.

Dreamers, all of us, dreamers. We older ones were more
Down-to-earth than the ones that came later, of course.
It was like raising three generations, Ma used to say. But
Dreamers, every one of us. Never once did both feet
Touch the ground. Reality was a rope to tether everyday minds,
Leon used to say. Not for us, Ma would remind me every day —
Certainly not for you.

It was Ma who was the dreamer. I had to work every day
Of my life; I never got to be a child. It was a miracle that
I made it through high school; and if Ma'd had
Any more babies, I'd probably never have finished. Most
Of us kids didn't. But I worked, and sometimes we had
Potato soup, and we older ones had to pretend
Not to be hungry. No wonder my generation overfed yours.

III.
Sometimes I had to go from house to house borrowing
Money from Ma's friend Tsurrah, paying back
Shlomo-with-the-big-hands what we owed him from last month.
I was the one they sent to do it — I was the oldest girl and
It was much too degrading for the boys, though they
Were older, bigger and stronger. Ma was busy with
The newest baby, or reading Edgar Guest, little poems
She cut from the newspaper, teaching herself
To read English.

We found some of the poems she must have especially liked
Tucked into her recipe books when we went through her things
After she died, dividing her memories among us: I want this
And I want that and Oh, my God, who'd have thought
She'd have saved... I remember that day so clearly,
Some of us hadn't called or written for months
And there we were, wanting something to remind us
That she was really ours, once.

IV.
Pa was too proud to think about money, Ma used to say.
He was too tired after selling stuff off a truck all day,
And too busy dreaming. I used to wonder what he had
To dream about, all day, sitting in the sun or the snow,
Calling "Fresh Fruits!" or "Rags for sale!" So I was the one
Who borrowed and repaid, friend to friend, month to month.
I hated it.

But even with reality landing us always on our feet,
What dreams we had! Every one of us, a dreamer. No food
Sometimes, but always, such dreams. There were
So many of us; and we were hungry, hungry. All of us,
Starving artists in some way. I don't think
Anyone's dreams came true.

The Cold Road

The Hudson is laced together like a Victorian dowager
sausaged in her corset, her flesh
pours over and beneath and between the stays.
The bridges crisscross each other over the river,
alternating asphalt and steel,
decorated by a smoky lace fischu,
the early morning fog that is sometimes a broken mist,
sometimes whole, solid. February breaks
beneath the girders, sheets of cloudy plate glass ice
discarded like a fractured life.
Like the iced river below the bridges, we are frozen,
following the road as if it led to July.

Schizophrenia

I.

A dentist's drill gone mad, it screeches
across my teeth, finds all the nerves
exposed, quivering like a lover
left unsatisfied. I go to see you, and

a stale bread fills my mouth
when we speak. Each word you stare through
is a choking, sharp-cornered bite
that turns my breath to mold.

I hold what I remember you to be
against my heart so I will not forget,
and as I drive home a keening escapes that
connects me to all loss, all time.

This came, sudden as ice.

II.

You are not really dead, though you tried to be.
It's just that a part of you is missing in action, and I wonder, where?
We share dinner and you tell me that someone is angry at Shakespeare
and has changed the conjunction in "to be or not to be:

to "to be *and* not to be" and that you understand this very well. I wonder
how you feel, hallucinating voices of never-lovers and devil-doers,
if you hear them all at once, if you believe them
only sometimes, if they argue non-stop, Shakespeare
and Van Gogh, Mötley Crüe and Twisted Sister. Are they real,
always with you,
always?

Just Like a High School Dance, Only Worse

The tiny tense smile begins to freeze my face
the minute the band begins to play. Cold Perrier
chills my hand through its plastic reservoir. I walk
the periphery of the floor, the borderland between carpet
and glossed wood, remembering advice from others like me:
to meet men's eyes and to smile at everyone.
I pose myself as if for flight
right near the door I had slipped in through,
graceful as the dancers stepping through routines
any Arthur Murray studio would recognize.

The band changes the rhythm, and a woman
in a black leather mini and too much turquoise eyeliner
turns a practiced foot over her partners in an intricate
step-cross-together-step-turn. A few of the others begin to pair,
and dance. Men walk by, stare up and down and up again.
One stops to tell me, "In a couple of months, you'll be ready."
I suddenly smell a slaughterhouse, fresh meat hanging
open and raw. A man asks me to waltz and I feel him
growing hard beneath his silk suit. He holds me tighter,
and I try to back off, like the woman Texas two-stepping
it away from the oily character tracking her down the center
of the dance floor. My partner has his routines perfected.
I feel inept, my body not my own, detached
after so many years being badly attached. Finally
he lapses into silence and the box-step, both of which
I can handle, till the end of the dance. He
returns me to the sidelines, tested and failed.

Others look me over, and I begin to examine my shoes,
fascinated, while I debate whether the ladies room or anywhere else
is safer than here. Instead of retreating, I grab my courage
as if it were a baseball bat and reconnoiter the edge
of the dance floor again, dump one full drink into a trash can
so I can purposefully move toward the bar
where the men congregate. Suddenly, in defense
or in defiance, I begin to return the up-down-up
appraisal and dismissal routine. It feels good.
I begin to miss the sound of my own voice
being intelligent, look for a conversation to start,

I stand back to back behind a legal type
in a three-piece pin stripe gabardine and last year's power tie,
eavesdrop on his male bonding ritual with another guy,
hoping one of them will talk to me. He's
an auto mechanic, drying out again. His ex-wife
drove him off the wagon. Everything is her fault.
I walk over to the lumberjack type growing roots in the corner,
chair tipped back against the wall. We stare at each other
and in the instant before I say hello,
I notice his unfocused eyes, dilated pupils, his breath
pushing too hard against his chest,
his deodorant not working.

As I go for my coat, I wonder
if, in some other world surrealistically paired to this,
singles court without desperation,
glide to "Let Me Call You Sweetheart," turning
in three-four time, like dolls on a music box,
or whether it's always like this.

Her Father

That's a dashiki she's wearing — orange, cream, red,
designed as though someone spilled mottled sunshine
across soft fabric back in 1965. It's faded —
not pseudofaded like the ones you get
at Not Fade Away, all bright and brittle and
don't-touch-me. This one is wrinkled and worn thin,
soft with age and smelling lightly of old pot.

She found it buried in the old trunk in the back
of her father's closet, where she also found
those funny wide-bottomed jeans
with the patches saying BAN THE BOMB
and PEACE. She puts it on with strange reverence,
not understanding why this is different from any
of his other shirts she's welcome to borrow.
She looks in the mirror on his door, thinks its "neat,"
can't figure out how to match PEACE and NONUKES
with his gray three-piece pinstripes,
the Rollex on his wrist, his Republican registration.

Smoke and Mirrors

I thought the pitch was meant
only for me. It flooded me, warmed
me like petals opening to May.
Gratitude, no easy heart to cross,
warned, "It's a lie, all done with
mirrors hidden on his heart. He
doesn't know the difference, doesn't
see you as one-in-the-world. He
doesn't even know your last name.
He's only a collector." This was
truth, bitter and harder to swallow
than pride.

I wanted to break his smile,
write my name in soap on his mirrors
and then wash them clean, but
six witnesses would each perceive it
differently, even as it happened. Each
would make him true, rewriting his history
along with mine, calling out, "You
needn't explain why!"

Anger reasons with me: do it as if
it were a secret! Don't tell him that
only you could write him out of your past,
erase his future! Don't tell him you
have your own tricks, all in the wrist, or
done with smoke.

The joke is, those witnesses: they'd
never guess why. They'd only know.

I Watch You Grow...
(For Karen)

You've come through hell.

Maybe some was invited by your teen drugging.
Maybe not. Others have done the same, without
The same result, but you —
You got caught.

Or maybe it was the loneliness that came first —
And the voices brought you company.
Maybe not. Or the strain of living in a family
Where you learned to expect too much from yourself.
Maybe it was too big a puzzle — parent's dreams
Conflicting with your vision of who you were.
Maybe not.

Maybe it was genetically just going to happen anyway,
Though I still ask, almost twenty years later,
Why to you — you of the loving heart, the trusting ways
And the exquisite caring?

But I have to be honest.
There has been benefit to this tortuous journey, this
Slow winding through trouble and calm.
It brought us close. I learned to understand your pain
Because you eloquently describe its insidious sliding
Around your mind. It brought you home to me,
Helped you discover how loved you are, both
Mother to daughter, and as two women traveling
This life together. I still wait to hear your voice tell me
That this has been a good day, so I can
Rejoice with you. Or this wasn't such a
Good day, so I can commiserate.

Today, you came through another storm, and
I take pride in your handling of almost all
Of your own situations. I am proud of
How you are making differences in your own life,
Of how you step forward to welcome yourself back,
Time and time again. Sometimes I hear the pain
In your voice, the fatigue, and I hold my breath
Till the sun starts to peek out again. And I notice that
The dark times are less frequent (if not always less dark),
And that they pass more quickly, that you handle them with
Greater and greater elegance. The mother side
Of me feels your growth, and inside myself
I hug you and let you go a little bit more,
With love, each time.

Mis-Match

So. You don't agree with me —
again. And as usual in this position,
your face begins to grow, filling the space
in front of my eyes with beard and red words
that suck the air away from me. Your eyes glow
hot, burn cold, widen, narrow, then steal the light.
Your lips begin to thin to slit lines, opening and closing
around sounds that bellow like a sperm whale's spray.
At the point where your jaw meets your neck, a
thick rhythm pulses hard. Your cheeks
pick up the beat and contract in and out in time.
It turns you into a blowfish, comic eyes bulging.
All of this happens in the instant my heart travels
from my throat to my stomach and back again.

The next minute I know I'm tired
of this old song and dance. You won't move, so
I pace back once, twice. My mind does
a fast push and you sail into space, shrinking
as you travel. I wash out your color and
you become an old tv set rerunning Eddie
Cantor, banjo-eyed and skipping around the stage,
going backward double-time, getting smaller.
I decide I like you like this, silent and nearly
gone. Tomorrow, it won't hurt to take out
my crayon and color you away.

Amazing Grace

Twilight smacks this room first. I
stare across the oranging carpet
at the old honky-tonk upright in the corner,
a lonely chunk of scarred mahogany
that sits at right-angled opposites
with the stereo components
beside it. It's aged well,
the real ivory keys
only vaguely yellowed
by what must have been
years of someones fingering.

I wonder if
I should have learned to play. It
might be soothing now, to sit
on the bench in a romantic organza
dress with a full skirt
swirled over the seat, a warm breeze
flowing through the Victorian sheers
at the window, wrapping the air
around me. I can see myself
in a soft-focus haze, graceful fingers
coaxing Debussy from the soundboard.

I look at my fingers, short and stub-nailed.
I should abandon the bench, I think,
give up the breeze and the filmy curtains,
stand in old jeans and a faded denim shirt. It
would feel good, I revise, to be pounding out
some old Jim Croce in the humid, solid-walled
heat of August's sundown, pouring
LeRoy Brown's life through my
blunt-ended fingers.

The CD clicks off. The room has turned
yellow-black, washed over by moonshadows.
I stare at the Cheshire-cat presence
that overlords this room, grinning its indifference.
The music I might have made
ghost-dances like dreams
backlit against the moon.

The Reality of You and Me

We saw him at a craft fair last year,
this old man in the baggy pants and
pilled gray cardigan. He had burn scars
on his hands, and a two-day beard-growth,
but he was so proud of being a creative artist
that it was hard to see beyond the glow on his face.

He made metal scenes from old tin cans,
scenes that he remembered or created freehand
(which may account for the burns) with a set of torches
his grandkids had given him as
a retirement present. Candles sat inside
the delicate, intricate settings
and the flames gave the designs a romantic,
Victorian feeling, like silhouettes
cut against a quivering October sunset.

"Look at this!" I held up a
rectangular park setting that was
likely once a container of imported olive oil. A boy
and a girl held hands amid a tangle of flowering vines.
A pair of oxy-acetylene blackened trees
threw out a few slender leafless branches that
grasped each other in a heart-shaped
frame around the couple.
"I can do that for you," you bragged. "Save me
some cans, and I'll burn you
a wonderland of holders for your candles."

I believed, then, in all your promises. For days
I cooked with canned goods, emptying
my pantry of potential art forms, my imagination
on fire. We stored the cans
on your back porch, waiting for
time and inspiration.

Yesterday, I saw an old man at the craft fair in the mall.
His hands were burned, and he made candleholders
out of tin cans. On the day I left, ours were still
choked with old motor oil, were glutted
with washers and nuts.

Portrait in Silver

His name's been Anglicized by now, changed
from something white man can't pronounce, and
he lives in an air-conditioned raised ranch
somewhere out there in the Southwest. He has the build
of an old-time seafarer, the barrel-chested,
thick-wristed kind that show up in late-night
black-and-white Wallace Beery movies.

His hammer grip hands are covered with
the black of oxidized silver, and splinters
of metal are imbedded so deeply in the whorls
of his fingers, they're part of his soul. His
jeans are shreds at the bottom, worn beyond
recognition of Wrangler or Lee, sucked to every curve
of his lower body, decorated by a python belt
caught by a buckle of turquoise, coral
and bear claw.

His hair, long and straight, is captured behind his back
by a leather thong rescued from a bolo
that never got made. His boots, black as his hair
used to be, are covered with dust; and his hair
is shot with the kind of gray that shines
like polished chrome in the sun. Everything about him
looks like his grandfather, like that man
whose fading sepia picture lies half-hidden
in the antique dresser that's buried in his attic.

He calls himself, generically, Native American:
it's the style to be grounded in a politically correct
cause these days. But his face bears the flat planes
and high cheekbones of the Navajo, and you can see
tribal pride lurking deep in his hooded eyes
and in the intricate craftsmanship
of the feathers and leaves that trademark
the jewelry he creates.

The Caretaker

Sumbitch, I werked fer that damn rich bastid
over thirty year, 'n then the friggin' jerk
goes an' cans m'ass with no warnin', no gold watch,
not e'em a Timex. Jest "git yer stuff
'n move on out, Jim. I'm sellin' the house. Here's
yer wages 'n a li'l sumpin' extra."

Well, I looked at the sumpin' extra, an' I wanted
real bad ta tear up the fuckin' check, but
it were ten thou' 'n I got the mor'gage on my place
'n the damn horses t' feed. Shee-it, I'm sher glad
the kids is growed 'n gone.

So, anyways, I figger, Jimbo, ya been a fuckin' good
keer-taker (that's what he calls me) 'n this
rich ol' bastid, he treated ya okay
'œpt fer no notice. Shee-it, he only used the damn
lakehouse summers 'n sumtimes not e'em then
these past coupla years. Ya werked hard, keepin' up
sumone else's stuff, but'cha got paid fair. Year 'round,
too. An' ya been yer own fuckin' boss
all them years, too. So now what'cha gonna do?
Go t'werk fer some dum-ass fac'try boss fer
less wages in a year than ya got
fer three monts fer this damn rich bastid?

Well, then I thinks ta m'self, Jimbo, y'stupid-ass jerk,
ya got th'house, built it real cheap (and mostly on his time, too)
'n ya got'cherself a good woman, 'n ya got them horses,
'n yer dogs. Sumbitch, just be grateful ya got'cher
right friggin' mind, 'n that wife o'yers rat-holed the money
she stole outta yer pants when y'was asleep,
e'em though ya give her hell fer it.

My Mary, she tells me, "Jimmy, ya got'cher health.
We got each other. Yer close t'sixty. Ya done good."
So I thought I'd ree-tire early 'n trade some horses,
mebbe do some fishin', fix a coupla mowers fer pocket cash.
Hell, I might even set down 'n cut out them fuckin' wood things
Mary likes to paint on, so's she cin sell 'em at the kids' diner.
People buy shit like that, y'know?

So now I'm ree-tired, like some classy-assed bastid,
'n I do fuckin' well what I want, when I want
kinda like before — ony now I don't git paid fer it,
'n I mostly ony have t'do fer the wife.
Mostly — shee-it — mostly
I drink...

The Arts Discussed in the Beauty Salon

I'm playing the Copeland Sonata,
you know, the one written about
the same time as that Appalachian stuff;
last movement's kind of nice —
all that jazzy violin
that slides around the scale

It's really a very appropriate piece
considering it was written in memory of
a violinist friend of his that died
and now I'm playing it
at the Dutch Reformed Church,
part of a memorial service
given by friends of this local violinist
who died
but no one can find the body

Copeland's music — very
Frederick Remington, Wyeth-like
(Newell, of course, not Andrew)
definitely American but a touch of English
too in theme and sound. I didn't realize
how Wyeth had died, hit
by a train when his car stalled
on the track and he refused to get out.
He'd had dreams of that sort of end,
his family reported later.

Horrible to die like that.
Are the curls too tight?

Stillborn

I wait for this poem
as if I were waiting
for the next pain. The
urge to push
is overpowering.
The urge to hold back
clenches my fists.
My back hurts.
I draw up my knees
And sit-squat in my chair,
half in, half out
of an image I can't imagine
the rest of.
The computer grunts.
No more will come. I
freewrite nonsense
across the page; water breaking
prematurely
has more sense than this.

Snowstorm

The pines that guard the house
bend under last night's heavy white,
old Atlases tired of their burdens.
Once they stood proud as new lovers;
weight meant nothing then. They
juggled seasons with a single shrug,
as if populations didn't depend
on the fingertip balance of gods
spinning planets through the air.
Last night, they played out the last
of their youths. Old age fell
fast and white across their shoulders.
Now they curve their backs
against the weight of tiny flakes
and wonder what went wrong.

She's Only Thirty

Almost young, but her thighs
hang over the sides of the chair
she sits in, and her breasts sag
toward her baggy gut, and
she's the study that proves
that gravity works. She chain smokes,
cooks cheap greasy food that she shares
with three kids underfoot and the roaches
that hide when company comes, all the while
she watches the soaps, feeling sorry
for the characters.

She had a husband once, who beat her
to show who was boss and to destroy
whatever she felt good about
that day. She lost her hearing after
one of those, and she forgot
what mattered. It got easy to
turn deaf ears away so she wouldn't
have to hear the instinct that told her
to run — just grab the crying babies
and run.

She stayed
till he flexed his muscles
at another victim. She threw out his
clothes, sold his cycle, and
bought herself a suitcase. One day he came back
to change his clothes and beat her once more.
She shot him with the gun he used to hide
in the bedroom closet.

Requiem for a First Love

Sometimes, I think I can write you,
draw images around you, at least
as you were then, so close
your mind seemed to go through me.
I could feel the lust/love/heat,
whatever it was, on my cheek
while we hung forever-promises
into the air like ornaments
for the gods. I seemed to drift
in little lapses of time
between your visits, only
I wondered why it was that
all the best I did was done
when we were apart. It was for you,
I thought. To make you proud, show you
I was creative, worthy.

My not being a part of you
didn't fit your plan. You took back
your ring, your promises, all
you thought you'd given me,
and gave in exchange
every bit of freedom
that you took for yourself. But
for months, it could have. . .
might have . . .
I should have . . .
if only I . . .
damn you, we never even fucked.

So many years later,
it's hard to know I had loved you
except
I can't write you here.

This Process
Portsmouth, NH 2001

I watch as you do this:

You charmingly cadge a lead pencil from an old woman passing by,
then search through the car for a good size piece of paper. You
settle on a white bag that held a piece of pottery
we'd purchased along the way, and
tear open the bag along the seams to make it bigger.

In your new pants and shirt, you lay down
on damp grass on top of an old grave.
You struggle with the wind that wants to rip your paper
from the 1709 headstone. You win.

You rub the lead over all the old letters that proclaim
the final property rights of someone you never knew
and who wasn't a family ancestor.
Genealogy might have given you a reason to do all this,
but you need no cause to put your hands on
something so old, or to connect somehow
to a life so far passed.

I watch you do this
while tattooed motorcyclists roar their steeds
over the low bridge beside the simple cemetery.
Local foot traffic ignores you —
just someone else doing the same old thing —
except for one young mother,
explaining to her fascinated toddler
what gravestone rubbing is. The child wants to know
if you're tickling a ghost.

Deeply immersed,
you miss all but the connection
to some past you imagine. You hear nothing —
you've left this world.

Old Men / Old Women

Old women have complaints to tell —
past surgeries, labor and childbirth,
how arthritis sets in and you need help
just to button your blouse. They whine —
why bother to dress, the children
never come to visit, and after all
they've done to raise them right, baked
those darned cookies even though
it was a chore just so the house
would smell cozy and chocolate. Taught
them their manners, their pleases
and thank you's — not that they ever
used them but at least they knew
they were supposed to. Now all you get
are flowers on Mother's Day
and a plant at Christmas, or another
bed jacket, and someone hired
to wipe your chin and that's supposed to mean
they love you. Well, you never can tell
till it's almost over what you
should have done, right?

Old men have stories to tell. Men
DID things back then, when a man
could BE a man — sweated
through summer's tortuous heat pounding
railroad spikes, digging foxholes
halfway across Europe, the Kaiser
so close you could smell the bratwurst
on his breath. Made an auto
that ran, b'gosh, almost thirty mile an hour —
and boy, didn't that just turn
the ladies' heads! Oh yeah, the old joints
ache a little, but ya feel the ache more
in here, in the heart. That's the one
that really grabs ya. The ache in the groin?
Hell, that's just an occasional half-hope
or maybe a good memory — but not as good
as working the mine or givin' 'em hell
over there!

The Day You Packed Your Bags and Left

We bought those flowers on our honeymoon,
thought that their yellows and oranges
would last forever, like sunshine and passion.
Why should we have thought anything different?
We were young, and as new as the flowers.

The blooms graced the windowsill for years,
Throwing their wild colors across the bed.
One day I noticed that they weren't real,
only cheap silk with raw edges, weak stems.

I had never seen them change. It was as if
they had suddenly grown dust in their secret folds.
Suddenly they faded like an arid, eroded landscape
warped by Dali. The glass you'd bought to hold them
had turned cloudy. That last day,
it cracked clear through.

Ganeshe
(Earthquake In India)

I hear the rumbling, feel the earth
tremble, and it is my father
all over again, wanting me to marry
for riches, to lose my Self to gold.
And his anger, when I will not,
shakes the world. My poor father,
when he learns that I cannot subscribe
to his values, is so angry he beheads me.
(Being a free-thinker has its dangers.) And
when he sees I have a point, he
is mournful, replaces my head
with that of an elephant. This is
quite an obstacle to overcome, and
I do that.

They begin to call me
the Remover of All Obstacles, but
I have no wish to become an idol.

And there is this shaking earth, reminding me
again how it was, terror in Bombay and
the losses in Poona. Someone else must have
angered my father; it isn't easy, being
offspring of Shiva.

"My people," I wish to plead, "please
my people, do not run." And then, I see it is
the earth shaking on its own, and I want
to run, too. But I stand here, heavy, weighted.
"I need to stand steady," I think. "These people
will come back and face many obstacles. I
must be a symbol for them." But I'd rather dance.

Learning the Hard Way

Clock ticking, hands spinning,
Wings attach themselves to hours.
DayPlanner filled, notes
Bursting out of their calendared squares,
I catch my breath, gasping for air
And dive in again
Offering up my time
Again, Again, Again
As if it — or I — had no value.

Surrounded by hospital pastels
I breathe bottled oxygen
As if I had all the time in the world.
My head full of cotton,
Fiberglass. Ideas tickling?
Someone else runs my day.
I rest and let it happen.
It all gets done.

Speed Kills
(for David Jr.)

You drive yourself through life, never looking
at the traffic around you, careen around days
berserk, like a Lotus out of control. Wind
pares flesh from bone — you have no time
to notice. There are no red lights
in this world, no limits, no brakes.
The road knows this.

Racing hard against the waves, you become
a boat throttled full into the sea, bow
almost vertical with desperation. Foam
crashes over your face; seaweed flies up
and tangles in your hair. Spray burns
your eyes, rolls like tears over
your cheeks. You follow a circle,
speeding nowhere over and over.
The sea knows this.

Ravel played at double speed, your notes pound
against each other like lovers, frenzied,
skin slapping skin. Bolero clashes beyond
music, beating harder, louder. The player
gives up and eats the tape, spits it out,
breaks the sound into silent shards.
The composer stops spinning
in his burial plot, grateful.
The music knows this.

And still you fight your way
toward balance, fly down the expert trail,
swoop, ride currents of air, a hawk with
no prey. Your skis point in opposite directions,
neither of them forward. You're sure you won't make it
around the next curve, much less
to tomorrow. There's no graceful way
to turn around, to do today again, better.
You are a shot arrow that will
never grace the target.
You know this.

Seeing Double Shadows

The moon shines on the quiet walkway
between buildings, throws shadows against
the granite curb. The furred edges blend
into a center where they solidify,
slowly become a compression of self.
Inside the concrete core is the deeper place,
where feelings darken, harden to polished obsidian.
I'm stone, cold as a glass pane in December
in Albany, borrowing emotions from the shadow
place that's left after what I remember
becomes what I forget.

Losing the Words

I can imagine how my father felt, the frustration —
knowing you know what you want to say, and not
finding the words to broadcast it. He would lie
in his bed, thumping his head with his fingers, repeating,
"the words, the words," leaving me to guess
what he wanted to talk about.

Just like when I was little, I never got it right.
No matter what I guessed, it wasn't what he wanted.
Old and frightened, his eyes asked me to find words for
what he wanted to say. A hospice worker asked him, just
before he lost all his words, what was his one regret. I held
my breath, wanting an apology for old sins, sins
for which no words could suffice except, "I'm sorry."
It wasn't what he said.   .

At the end, when he was lying cold, silent and
beyond words or knowledge of them,
I whispered in his ear,
"I forgive you anyway."

Denial Was Always Your Ace in the Hole

I used to say that if we had met someplace, say,
a committee or something, we'd never be friends.
But you were my mother, so we did our
co-dependent dance in some sort of lock-step
rhythm, me never meeting your expectations and
you never meeting my needs. You turned cold,
stubborn; I turned away.

A hundred years later, you needed me and I saw
to it you were cared for. And when you drew your
last breaths, I was there, holding your hand,
giving you permission to go, waiting with you.
You hadn't recognized me in years, had
rendered me invisible by simple denial. Your
brain didn't register me, my father's death, or
any of your gone family. At 79, you slid back
into your twenties, before I was born, before
you were married, to when you were happy
and looking ahead, where you always
remembered things best.

Denial was always your ace in the hole.
You were an expert at saying no and
looking the other way, as if it were some great
grace to be able to ignore, or
see nothing amiss.

You became the long-suffering, your sighs
would ice the room as you told everyone how fine
everything was. It became my
game to discover where the truth was hidden,
and if you knew it or if you were lying
to yourself as well.

Like the time I came home from school,
pregnant by a boy you hated, how you planned
my shot-gun wedding and told the world
what a fine son I'd brought you. I can
still see your teeth clench around that one.
Or the time my father had an affair and you made
"that Bono woman" the whispered ax you
held over his head for years after it was over,
all the while smiling and telling the family
how wonderfully perfect your life was.

Denying your anger gave you cramps in
your early years, cancer as you grew older. I
watched your jaw lock tighter and tighter, till
your lips disappeared in a hard line and your brow
furrowed deep with the concentration
of holding it all in. Now gone, your truth
doesn't matter — mine does. And when I die,
mine won't matter either.

This Rocking Sweetness
(for D.G.)

I thought it would be
just something quick and fun,
mutual pleasure shared
with no yesterday, no tomorrow.
And the truth of it is, that's it.

I didn't expect
the sunshine of gentle hands
moving like butterflies over my skin,
nor the rocking sweetness of caring
that went on for one moment more.
The surprise was that it mattered to you
that I was held so close to your heart
our skin melted away, that
you created for me a special space
cocooned in your arms, that
you didn't rush away, abandoning me
to the brittle crack of night.

What matters now is that for a while,
I was a precious gift to you; and
that you made me know it.

What matters now is that I'll have
this smiling gift
forever.

After 9/11/01: Terrorism
Is Some Action That Alters
How You Are the Rest of Your Life

Terrorism is the rest of my life,
remembering. It creates awful changes,
and what I once took for granted
never can be again. Like the hijackers
who guided planes into NYC's twin towers,
killing thousands, leaving body parts and the smell
of death over everything, leaving the country
feeling open and vulnerable, untrusting.

Or my father's touches that came unbidden
and unwanted in my childhood night,
the smell of rancid gin and stale cigarettes
heavy on my face, wanting to retch
and wrench myself away, but
not knowing that I could. How each night
I was afraid, untrusting. How that turned
into ice and singularity, even now, when
I feel threatened. How it took years
to remember, yet it was always so
close to the surface. And when I chose to
recall it, how it devastated me for years after.

Terrorism is raw, even after it heals.
The wounds lie ready to bleed when scratched,
and the itch is always there. The wondering,
the non-sense of it. The remembering.

Peeling Back the Layers

We tear our house apart, surrendering
The artifacts of our lives to the
Guests we invite into our garage.
Glittered signs, clever ads, and
Smiling assurances that
"Yes, that works just fine" are
Beacons to the outside world
That yet another family is either
Moving out or falling apart.

Chaos reigns. What once had a place,
No longer does. Pieces of our lives
Float or limp through the house, heading
Toward a table in the garage,
Preparing for some squinty-eyed
Neighbor to denigrate its value
By asking "can you do any better?"
As if our oak coffee table
In perfect condition wasn't worth
Even the $20 we offer it at.

This is not where I want to be,
Sitting beside my garage door
At the cold end of October, waiting
For someone to decide if the layers
Of our lives hold any value,
Or interest. Like when my parents died,
And their possessions, the gifts they gave
To each other and to the marriage,
The gifts they worked hard and saved for,
Went into the garage sale
For pennies on the dollar.

You have to wonder at times like those,
And times like this, if any of it was worth
The getting, and the caring for, and the keeping.
I'm sensing now what I sensed then: that I'd prefer
To give it all away to worthy people rather
Than bear this insult of strangers' hands
Rummaging, dealers' eyes judging, or
Rasping voices trying to bargain me down
Another quarter.

Spring

Buds begin to expose their green, tentative
as a lover left suddenly behind after the affair
has ended. Winter frost had stretched ice
over his heart. He'd thought himself
dead, gone to old sticks, brittle,
snapping apart in the wind.

Today the sun pours a gray light, but
it is light, nevertheless. His heart
begins to move, stiff at first, like the thawing
sticktrees at the boundary of lake and shore.
Today the water breaks the ice, a
wild gust over the dam he'd made
of his heart. Next month, he will deny
winter ever existed.

A New Music

Today
I saw   pieces   of myself
in you,   things
that disturbed me   about me.
I never thought much   before now
how well I could have justified
staying   together
glued partners   in a dance
neither liked.   I'm not fond of rearranging
my music   to match someone else's
rhythm.

Today
I saw   an old me
in you,   readjusting   to match
or manipulate   the music.   Being
the conductor   may equal survival,
but   it's lonely.   I saw you
look in the mirror,   your eyes
repeating themselves,   looking like mine.
Your tempo   became   syncopated,
unpredictable.   I had never
seen myself
like that before.

In one beat,
the sudden   surprise reality:
that when you dance,   you are
vulnerable,   that you
fear the pain   accepting this would bring.
We really are nice people,   you know,
you and I.   We deserve
brighter music,
livelier jazz.

Meant To Be Coupled

There is an energy that gets
generated when we set our minds
to something, hearts tuned in to the
big picture, with our focus upon that
one step ahead, together. It's a
swirling sensation that lightens my head
like a blood pressure drop when I
suddenly stand up. All you have to do
is be there, into the project with me,
and I experience this. Walk into the room,
ready, and immediately I am a glad shambles.
It excites me to have you ready and eager
to create something with me. Times like this,
even our stumbling together is like laughter.
Alone, I am halted, lame, capable
but slow to achieve. Well-partnered, I am
agile, a jumper taking hurdles smoothly.
It occurs to me that I am built for
teamwork, meant to be coupled, to pull
two-to-a-harness.

Taking Off the Masks

One by one, the masks come off the walls. The
Africans leave black ovals where they used to rest, the
French seem befuddled, as if caught in some language they
don't understand. The Balinese are just happy
to go somewhere else, and the little Indonesian
over the bed wonders if she will be happy in her new home.

I can tell you about the happy goddess, who shattered
into a hundred ceramic pieces the day my husband left.
How she started giggling the day he announced his unhappiness
and didn't stop till he packed and moved, when
she roared with laughter till she rocked herself right off the wall,
launched herself through the bedroom window, and fell apart on
the cinder block drip-line two stories down.

I can tell you about the wise-woman who watched
as I packed what remained of his belongings and left them
by the door to which I had changed the locks. I can tell you
about the wizard that held out his hand to halt my mental
laundry list of what I imagined I'd done wrong, then
transmuted it into all that I'd done right, held it up
like a mirror for me to see myself in.

I can tell you about the four elements that I made myself
of driftwood, plaster gauze and paste jewels, one representing
fire, one for air, one for water, one for earth. They remind me
to keep passion alive in my heart, to breathe deeply, to
move with the flow of whatever is, and to stay grounded. Or
the one I made of my partner — a white, watchful presence
guarding my sacred space, protective yet not disruptive.

These spirits I pack away carefully, one by one, to clear their energy
and make them ready for their new home. Removing the masks
from the walls bares the soul of my house. This house holds
too many memories of happiness and hurt, ordinariness and genius.
For years it has hidden its own pain and imperfection behind
a mask of furniture polish, paint and
manicured shrubbery.

Portrait

Unwittingly, I'm sure,
Anne Marie Eastburn
painted my portrait. Granted,
the painted figure is longer,
leaner, more fully busted and
exquisitely sexy — and I
am decidedly grayer, more jaded,
and living proof that gravity works.

But this me on the canvas — this
is who I am. Welcoming my own strength, and
joyously announcing myself to the world, I
blossom white and new, a lotus
with roots in the mud, strong stem,
growing beyond my past, arms
open to tomorrow.

Evvie

Working on the car, changing plugs and wires,
grease on my hands so thick I can't feel. When
I go inside and wash up, I see my hands for
the first time in years. I don't think I've noticed them
since Evvie used to hold them to her breasts, smiling
at how smooth they felt against her skin.

I've used these meathooks every day. They're
tools, like hammers, or they were weapons back in
those times when I drank too much and someone
talked to me wrong. That was a lifetime ago, too,
when I was young, and passion ran hot, right
or wrong.

I guess Evvie wouldn't smile at their smoothness now.
The skin is spotted and callused, knuckles swollen.
But this minute, washed and clean of auto grease,
I hold my great-granddaughter close, and
think of what Evvie and I started — this child
of the softest skin, holding my old fingers
in her trusting grasp.

Albany, NY: Two Cities

The first dockworker shouts a name
that shatters the frosted silence of
the hazed world where cold air and
the river-that-flows-both-ways
comingle and bruise the docks.
In the hour of magic when light waves
away the last wink of darkness, the soft lines
of the city begin to harden. Pink clouds
bump the fog, dry-brush the edges of steel.
Bananas are offloaded; the sun shines
yellower on their skins. The day burns
the corners of the world, turns the city
bright and brittle, the water brackish.
The city rushes through the day, wishing
for night. The battered docks wait for dawn,
new treasures, the eating sun.

First Homecoming
(for Barry)

Your beard is the color of mud. You've
punched holes in your ears and poked
silver hoops through, two on one side, one
on the other. You smile your hello and
I hold my breath, take note of your jeans,
strategically torn and tight, and of
your medium-size shoulders that are a
hanger for the 3X shirt that balloons
around your body, as if to say how much
you've missed me.

I divide immediately and half of me listens
in surprise to the mother-half telling you
you need a haircut. After two days, the half
of me that wore flowers wound in her hair
and marched anti-war over most of New York
state comes out of a quarter-century of hiding,
thinking that the earrings really do look good,
that you've grown handsome with the beard
and long hair.

I won't tell you because you probably
won't want to hear it; so I quietly admire you.
Both halves cross my fingers.

Mourning the Second Beatle

Dead of cancer at 58, and I think
how much closer this is to 79, the age
each of my parents chose to die, than it is to 1963,
to "All My Lovin'," the song they
interrupted to announce the assassination of JFK.

I think to myself that this man was still young, that
talent like his shouldn't be allowed to leave
so early, that there should be a contract at birth
requiring that a candle with such lively flame
not be allowed to melt too fast. It wasn't the same
when Crosby or Sinatra died; they were old, ready,
and not part of my generation.

I am surprised by my own tears, surprised that
emotion runs deep. What comes up for me is
the 20 years in which he won't make music. Like
John Lennon, gone before his time. Like
ideas that never get realized.

Statuary

"The sound of idols breaking
is a very private noise."
— Neil Simon

You ignored the sculpture
I had made of you, chiseled
your profile hard, and
turned your eyes to stone
that focused on some horizon
other than mine. You looked down
on me from your rock-core
angularity, until I learned
that hiding in your shadow
was as cold as the agate
of your eyes.
You fell from your pedestal
so quietly
no one could hear it.

The Pieces Left Behind

Moving out of this old place, I
circle round and round in crazy knots,
remembering. When you left this house,
you left almost everything to me, left
me with the furniture we chose together,
the memories, the box of photos, the
attachments, as if what we'd gathered
to set our stage had no more importance.

I should have followed your example
much earlier. But unable to recreate myself,
as you could, I kept this house and
all the assorted momentos, souvenirs
from a past that no longer had value,
daily reminders of our mutual failure.
Believe me, it isn't a blessing to
remember so well.

Today, I apologized to you, for whatever part
(however small) my actions might have played
in our demise. It was a good thing to do.
I leave this geography clean, letting the memories
fall away from me like those styrofoam "peanuts"
that fill packing boxes, falling away from
whatever's in the box when you pick it up, a few
good, hardy pieces left behind.

The Poet & the Line From Left Field

He didn't really know where the line came from, it just seemed to come
from left field. He tries hard to make it fit into the poem: adjusts
images, changes syntax, cuts off punctuation, but the line
still reads hot and smooth as mercury bursting through the end
of a thermometer.

No sacrifice would be too great to save it, so
he chops off the head of the poem and immediately apologizes,
tries to make it better by gluing the words back into place. The poet
adores the language of the line as much as he loves
the body of his poem.

He changes the bedding of adjectives, similes, metaphors
everywhere around it to make the atmosphere right. The line
purses its lips and mocks him; it laughs till
the whole poem rocks on the edge
of madness.

He can take no more; his red pencil slashes off the feet, but
the poem runs on. He tries to chase it down; he
loses his breath. He stops, struggles on sips of air that turn
to gasps, to long gulping sobs. Remorseful, the poet
patches its feet with splints and tape.

Now he slashes at the line itself, trying to show it
who is master. He cuts it to noun, to verb, to shreds, till it's gone;
but the poem will never be the same. It has known beauty, and evil,
and suffering, and will feel its bruises every time it's read.
The line is not dead.

It lies in pieces in the poet's basket. It lies with discarded ideas
and useless phrases, gathering an angry sorrow. It begins
to pull itself together again. Flames leap out of the words, devouring
the paper, the basket, the office,
the poet.

Throwing Your Voice at the Horizon

I was bike riding as a child with Sandy Shriro
off the high cement wall on Cumberland Ave
that separated the Rabbi's house from the rest
of the block. My bike rolled up into mid-air
and Death made a sudden lunge, long pink tongue
lizard-licking over the sharpest teeth
you ever saw. I was glad I had sent away
to an ad in Katy Keene comics so I could
amaze my friends and be the first on my block.
I threw my voice at Death, and knocked him
right between the eyes. Surprised or not,
Death vanished, only to reappear in my dreams
last night.

"Columbus was wrong," Death said.
"The world is flat." Now that the end is
more in sight, I'm not sure who to believe.
And Death by now must know for sure
that old ventriloquist trick.

When Sedona Sleeps

she curls around herself, a
dark glowing presence, safe
and deep in the valley

when Sedona sleeps, red rocks
guard her slumber, clouds
outlined by moonlight send
dreams, visions of tomorrow's sun,
patterns of light and
shadow, peace

when Sedona sleeps, Coconino
guards her, offers a celebration
of magic   moonbeams
dance the earth around her
breezes cool the air

A Son's Portrait of His Father

Someday a son
will draw his father's face
too guarded, his eyes
too wary, his smile
too rare. Nothing
will come easy to the boy
who is his father.
He will look at an old photo
and wonder if it's a mirror,
and which one of him is real.

Pleating the Days Into Folds

There are days when my life seems
to gather itself into little knife-edged pleats
that fold in and out like moments
remembered and forgotten. Days like this
are gold, or are rubble, depending
on the parts recalled, or the intensity of
recollection. Like the years I believed
you loved me, before I discovered
you also loved some man. Years later,
the occasional flashback on betrayal
still feels like a sucker punch
to my midsection with a baseball bat.

That discovery threw me down
a different reality, one in which
trust dropped out of my vocabulary. Balancing
myself between your days of abusive insults
and your nights of ignoring me became
a puzzle to be worked out in the spare time
I tried not to have, since the question was always
how many eggs I'd have to walk on today
to protect myself and our children from
your screaming fits, your razor sarcasm.

Today, whole and happy without you as I am,
I still mourn the young dreams I thought we had
together; the potential that was such
a blatant and seductive lie,
the hardest part to let go of.

Running on Premium & I Still
Can't Get the Lead Out

I'm at the health club, working it out
like the ads tell me to do, trying to remake
myself into firm curves and muscled lines,
and all the time I'm sweating and aching toward
that sexy, good-health glow, my head
is hollering at me about how you can
only teach old muscles to play dead. The
inside of my mind falls asleep while I do enough sit-ups
to make Jane Fonda jealous. A voice inside
asks why I'm doing this; another voice continues
to count leg presses as if they were sheep.
My eyes defocus and the lids droop.
Wherever I am, it's not here
or anywhere nearby. Maybe I'm on a parallel plane,
dragging myself through twice the day
two times harder than anyone else.

Being Samimi

A dream almost within reach is a miracle
but for that last agonizing stretch, fingers
straining, heart pounding. It's like being
samimi over the desert, rain pouring down,
aching to kiss the earth, evaporating
in the air before touch-down.

CrystalWings Publishing